Foundations in RE

Islam

essential edition

Foundations in RE

Islam

Ina Taylor

essential edition

Text © Ina Taylor 2001

Original line illustrations © Nelson Thornes Ltd 2001

The right of Ina Taylor to be identified as author of this work has been asserted by her in accordance with the Copyright, Designs and Patents Act 1988.

All rights reserved. No part of this publication may be reproduced or transmitted in any form or by any means, electronic or mechanical, including photocopy, recording or any information storage and retrieval system, without permission in writing from the publisher or under licence from the Copyright Licensing Agency Limited. Further details of such licences (for reprographic reproduction) may be obtained from the Copyright Licensing Agency Limited, 90 Tottenham Court Road, London W1P 0LP.

First published in 2001 by:
Nelson Thornes Ltd
Delta Place
27 Bath Road
Cheltenham
GL53 7TH
United Kingdom

01 02 03 04 05 / 10 9 8 7 6 5 4 3 2 1

A catalogue record for this book is available from the British Library.

ISBN 0-7487-5719-8

Printed and bound in China by Dah Hua Printing Press Co. Ltd

Page layout by Ann Samuel
Illustrated by Jane Taylor and Barking Dog
Picture research by Sue Sharp

Dedication
For Amrine and Rohila

Note: Throughout the series BCE (Before Common or Christian Era) and CE (Common or Christian Era) have been used in place of the traditional BC and AD. The new terms are more acceptable to followers of non-Christian religions.

Acknowledgements

With thanks to the following for permission to reproduce photographs and other copyright material in this book:

Courtesy of Al-Hidaayah Publishing and Distribution 9, 10, 42; Associated Press 36, 39, 53; Circa 12, 21, 59; Haj & Umra Travel Limited 64; Sonia Haliday 37; Islamic Relief 47; PA Photos 56; Peter Sanders 7, 13, 14, 18 (right), 20, 24, 25, 26, 27, 32, 38, 40, 50, 51, 55, 60, 62, 65, 66, 67 (bottom), 69 (top); Martin Sookias 18 (left), 22, 23, 28, 31, 33, 34, 35, 44, 46; Ina Taylor 41, 54, 57, 58, 69 (bottom); Trip 43, 45, 63, 67 (top).

Every effort has been made to contact copyright holders. The publishers apologise to anyone whose rights have been inadvertently overlooked, and will be happy to rectify any errors or omissions.

Contents

Unit 1 Beliefs
1.1	Symbols of Islam	6
1.2	Beliefs about God	8
1.3	Prophethood	10
1.4	The importance of the Qur'an	12
1.5	Akhirah	14
1.6	Five Pillars of Islam	16
1.7	Extension tasks	18

Unit 2 Worship
2.1	Preparation for prayer	20
2.2	Prayer positions	22
2.3	The Qur'an	24
2.4	Extension tasks	26

Unit 3 Mosque
3.1	The mosque outside	28
3.2	Mosque – prayer hall	30
3.3	Other rooms at the mosque	32
3.4	People at the mosque	34
3.5	Extension tasks	36

Unit 4 Living Islam
4.1	Family life	38
4.2	Halal and haram	40
4.3	Ramadan	42
4.4	Id	44
4.5	Concern for others	46
4.6	Extension tasks	48

Unit 5 Rites of Passage
5.1	Birth ceremonies	50
5.2	Marriage – preparation	52
5.3	Marriage – ceremony	54
5.4	Death, funerals and mourning	56
5.5	Extension tasks	58

Unit 6 Holy city of Makkah
6.1	Life of Muhammad	60
6.2	Receiving the Qur'an	62
6.3	Hajj 1	64
6.4	Hajj 2	66
6.5	Extension tasks	68

Glossary 70

1.1 Symbols of Islam

Islam is one of the six big religions. The Arabic word Islam means to **obey** God. People who follow Islam are called **Muslims**. There are over two million Muslims in Britain.

The start of Islam

Islam began in a desert country. The most important messenger was Muhammad. He was born in Saudi Arabia in 570 CE.

If you are in the desert, it is hard to find your way. There is sand everywhere. It all looks the same. In the day it can be too hot to move about. People often travel at night. They used to look up at the stars to work out where they were.

The symbol of Islam is a crescent moon and a five point star.

Some people use the night sky like a map. They can work out which way to go.

6 Beliefs

Five point star

In the desert stars are the only fixed points. Muslims said Islam is like a star. It will **guide** people in life. The Muslim **star** has five points. Five is an important number in Islam. There are five things a Muslims must believe. These are called the Five Pillars of Islam (see page 16). Muslims must also pray five times a day.

Crescent moon

The moon is useful to people who travel at night. It gives them light to see where they are going. Muslims believe their religion will show them the way through life. A crescent moon is like the letter C. It is the new moon and will grow in size. Muslims hope their religion will also grow. In Islam each month begins with a new moon.

The symbol of Islam can be seen decorating some mosques.

Can you remember?

1. The word Islam means to _____ God.
2. People who follow the religion of Islam are called _____.
3. The symbol is a crescent moon and a _____ with five points.
4. Islam will _____ a Muslim through life like the stars guide them in the desert.

Do you know?

Why is the moon useful to people in the desert?

1.2 Beliefs about God

There is no God but Allah

This is the most important belief in Islam. Allah means God in **Arabic**. Muslims say there is only **one** God, he is called Allah. He does not have a son. Allah was not born. Allah cannot die. There is nothing or no one else like Allah.

Allah the creator

Muslims believe Allah made everything in the world. God also made everything in outer space. It was all made in six days. Everything has a meaning.

Allah makes people

Allah also made **people**. They were Allah's most important creation. Muslims believe Adam was the first man. Allah made him from clay, then breathed life into him. Allah made other men and women. Then Allah gave them rules about how to live. Allah said that if people followed the rules they would be happy. They would go to Paradise when they died. The word **Muslim** means a person who obeys Allah.

The Qur'an says, 'Have you not seen how everyone in heaven and earth glorifies God, even to the birds lined up in flight? Each knows its prayer and how to glorify Him. God is aware of whatever they do. God holds control over heaven and earth; to God is the final return'.

Allah knows everything

Muslims say Allah is very powerful. Allah knows everything. Allah knows what happened in the past as well as the present. He even knows what will happen in the future. Muslims say that everything we do is part of Allah's plan.

You choose

Muslims do not think we are puppets. They say we are free to choose what to do. But God already knows what we will choose.

Muslims use 99 different Arabic names to describe the many qualities of Allah. These are shown on this poster.

Can you remember?

1 Allah is the _____ word for God.

2 Muslims believe there is only _____ God.

3 The word _____ means a person who obeys Allah.

4 _____ were the most important part of God's creation.

Do you know?

Do Muslims think you are free to choose what to do next year?

1.3 Prophethood

What is a prophet?

A prophet is like a postman. He brings **messages**. The messages are from Allah.

A prophet is a person:
- who leads a good life.
- who can perform miracles.
- who never says the words are his own. He will say they are from Allah.

Prophets are very important in Islam. Muslims pay them great respect. When the name of a prophet is said, a Muslim will say, 'Peace be upon him'. They write pbuh after the name. Or they write the Arabic words for it as shown below:

Prophets in Islam

Muslims think Allah has sent many prophets in the past. There may have been as many as 200,000 prophets. But their names have been forgotten. This poster shows 25 prophets. There are **five** great ones. They include Jesus and Muhammad.

The message

All the prophets have said the same thing. People must only worship Allah. They must obey Allah's rules. Prophets have also told people:
- more about Allah.
- more about life after death.
- what Allah wants people to do.
- how to live a good life.

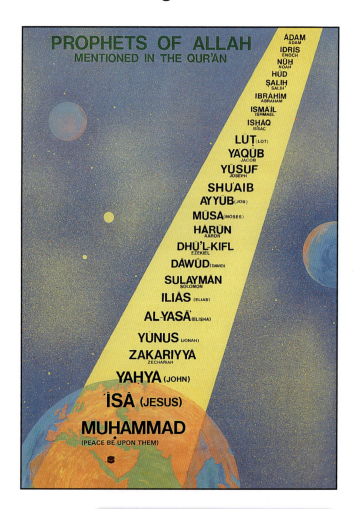

This poster lists the prophets named in the Qur'an.

Muhammad

Page 60 has more information about Muhammad's life.

> **He is the Messenger of Allah and the Seal of the Prophets.**

Muhammad was the most important prophet. He was a real person who lived around 600 CE. Muslims say Muhammad was the **last** messenger sent by Allah. He sealed, or closed off, the messages from Allah. Muhammad was given a holy book by Allah. This was his miracle.

This flag of Saudi Arabia states the most important belief in Islam. It says in Arabic, 'There is no God but Allah and Muhammad is the messenger of God'.

Can you remember?

1 A prophet brings _____ from Allah.

2 There are _____ great prophets in Islam.

3 _____ was the greatest prophet in Islam.

4 Muslims believe he was the _____ messenger Allah sent.

Do you know?

What miracle belongs with Muhammad?

1.4 The importance of the Qur'an

What is the Qur'an?

The **Qur'an** is the holy book for Muslims. The Qur'an was given to **Muhammad**. Muslims believe it has the exact **words** Allah gave to the people. They believe Allah has given people other holy books before, but mistakes have crept into those. Some of the books have even been lost. Muslims think Allah will not send any more holy books to people. The Qur'an is the final message from Allah.

No mistakes

The words in the Qur'an have been passed on carefully. No mistakes have got into it. Allah gave the Qur'an to Muhammad in Arabic. Muslims think they should read it in Arabic. If it is put into another language, the meaning might get muddled. Muslims must learn some **Arabic** so they can read the Qur'an.

Copies of the Qur'an are treated with great respect. The book is read on a stand.

Rules for life

The Qur'an teaches Muslims about:
- Allah.
- how a Muslim should behave towards Allah.
- what to do in everyday life.

Muslims believe the Qur'an has all the answers a person needs in life. They say new things may be invented, but people don't change.

Some Muslim countries use the rules in the Qur'an for their laws.

Making beautiful copies of the Qur'an is a way of pleasing Allah.

Can you remember?

1 The _____ is the Muslims' holy book.

2 The Qur'an contains the _____ of Allah.

3 It was given to the prophet _____.

4 Muslims have to learn _____ in order to read the Qur'an.

Do you know?

Why do Muslims like to read the Qur'an in Arabic?

1.5 Akhirah

> To God we belong and to Him we will return.

Muslims believe people were made by Allah. When they die they will go back to Allah. What a person does on earth matters. It is a test. It affects what happens to them when they die. Muslims believe in life after death. They call it **Akhirah**.

Day of Judgement

Muslims believe that people will be **judged** at the end of time. Their body and soul will unite. Then the person will stand before Allah.

Angels will give Allah a book. The book will have everything a person did, said or thought. Allah will judge if the person can go to Paradise or Hell.

The Qur'an says Paradise is like a beautiful garden. These gardens were made by Muslims in Spain.

Beliefs

The garden

The Arabic word for Paradise means **garden**. The Qur'an says Paradise will be beautiful. There will be flowers and shady trees. People will walk by fountains. They will rest in the shade. There will be lots of tasty fruits to pick. It will be peaceful. All the time people will grow nearer to Allah.

The place of fire

The Arabic word for Hell is fire. The Qur'an says people who disobey Allah will go to Hell. They will suffer. Boiling oil and molten metals will burn them. That will make them pure. Then they can go to Allah.

Hell is thought to be a place of great heat and pain.

Can you remember?

1 Muslims use the word _____ to mean life after death.

2 They believe people are _____ at the end of time.

3 _____ have a book that tells Allah what everyone has done in their life.

4 Muslims believe Paradise will be like a beautiful _____.

Do you know?

What do Muslims think will happen to them in Hell?

1.6 Five Pillars of Islam

There are five things that hold up the religion of Islam. They are called **pillars**.

1	**Faith**	Muslims believe there is one God. Muhammad is his messenger.	4 **Fasting**	Muslims do not eat or drink in the day for one **month** every year.
2	**Prayer**	Muslims must pray five times a day.	5 **Pilgrimage**	Muslims must try to go to **Makkah** at least once in their life.
3	**Charity**	Muslims should give 2.5% of their earnings to charity every year.		

Can you remember?

1. The five important beliefs of Islam are called _____.

2. The first one is most important. It is called _____.

3. Muslims fast for one _____ every year.

4. They must try to go to _____ before they die.

Do you know?

Why do you think these beliefs are called pillars?

1.7 Extension tasks

1. True or false?
   a) Islam began in England.
   b) Muhammad is the most important messenger in Islam.
   c) The sun and the moon are the symbols of Islam.
   d) Muslims must pray five times a day.
   e) A Muslim must go to Makkah once in their life.

2.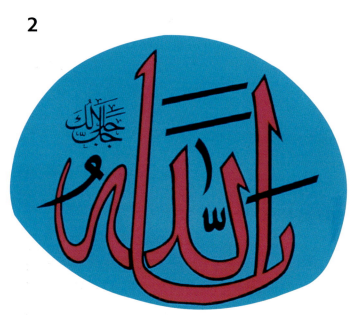

   This says Allah in Arabic. Copy this into your book. Write the English word next to it.

3. Trace or print a map of Saudi Arabia.
   Make sure Makkah and Madinah are marked. (They may be spelt slightly differently.)

4. In pairs or in groups of three make a poster of the **Five Pillars of Islam**.
   - You could roll paper to make a pillar for a 3D poster.
   - Put the name under each pillar.
   - Write a sentence about each pillar.

5. These are Muslim prayer beads. There are 99 beads on this string. Each one stands for a name of Allah. You can see the names on page 9. Write two sentences about the beads in your book.

6 Read each of these lines from the Qur'an. Choose the best one for this picture. Copy the words into your book carefully.

a) 'God knows everything.'
b) 'To God belongs the East and the West. Whichever way you turn there is the face of God.'
c) 'God is the light of the heavens and the earth.'

7

Try this role play:
A radio reporter talks to a person who has just become a Muslim. The reporter wants to know what they believe in now.

8 • Look up the flags of five Muslim countries. They have the symbol of Islam on them.

• Copy the flags into your book. Colour them correctly.

• Write the name of each country by the flag.

9 Match each word on the left to its meaning on the right. Copy the correct pairs into your book.

Islam	the holy book for Muslims.
Muslim	the name of God.
Qur'an	the messenger of God.
Muhammad	the religion of Muslims.
Allah	a person who follows Islam.

2.1 Preparation for prayer

'Prayer is the essence of worship', said Muhammad.

Muslims think the way to please Allah is to pray. Prayer is the second pillar of Islam. Every Muslim must pray **five times** a day. This shows a Muslim obeys Allah.

Muslims must do three things before they start:

- have a clean body, mind and space.
- be in the right frame of mind.
- use all their **mind** and body.

Clean mind and body

Muslims must cover their body for prayer. That is their head, arms and legs. Then they must **wash**. There is a special way of washing. It is to show Allah they want to be pure. They must not talk as they wash. Their whole mind must be on Allah. They say a prayer as they wash.

Special washing before prayer is called wudu.

20 Worship

The prayer rug

Muslims need a clean place to pray. They must face **Makkah**. A prayer rug is used to make the place clean. But Muslims can use any clean material. Designs on the rug help Muslims think about worship.

- there is an arch. This must point towards Makkah.
- a lamp hangs down the centre.
- some rugs have a mistake. It means only God is perfect.
- some have a scene of the Ka'bah (see page 66).
- the city of Madinah may be on the rug as well.
- there are no people or animals on it. Plants and flowers are used.

Can you remember?

1 Muslims must pray _____ _____ a day.

2 They need to face the holy city of _____.

3 Muslims must use their _____ and body in prayer.

4 Muslims _____ in a special way to show God they want to be pure.

Do you know?

Why do Muslims pray to Allah?

2.2 Prayer positions

The prayer movements are called rak'ahs. The word means **bending**. A Muslim bends to show he or she obeys Allah. Men and women pray in the same way.

1 The person stands at the **back** of the mat. He puts his hands by his ears. This shows he is listening to Allah.

2 He bows to show respect to Allah. He says, 'Glory to my Lord, the Great'.

3 He kneels and puts his head down to the floor. This shows that Allah is great. He says, 'Glory to my Lord, the Highest' three times.

22 Worship

4 The Muslim sits back on his heels. He has finished the rak'ahs. Now he can say a private prayer. He finishes by **blessing** the people on either side.

Friday prayers

All Muslim men try to go to the mosque for prayers on Friday. It makes them feel part of the **brotherhood** of Muslims. They can hear a talk from the imam, their teacher.

Can you remember?

1 The prayer movements are called rak'ahs because the word means _____.

2 A Muslim stands at the _____ of the mat to do the rak'ahs.

3 When a Muslim looks to each side, he is _____ the people next to him.

4 Muslims feel part of the _____ of Islam when they pray together.

Do you know?

How do Muslims show Allah is greater than they are?

2.3 The Qur'an

Respect for the Qur'an

Muslims believe the **words** of Allah are in the Qur'an. They pay the book great respect. Muslims can only touch the Qur'an if they have done wudu (see page 20). They must focus their mind before they start.

The Qur'an is put on a stand to be read. It must not be put on the floor. When the Qur'an is being read, no one talks. No one will eat or drink in the same room. The book is wrapped in a clean cloth when the reading is finished. Then it is put on the **top** shelf.

Learn it by heart

Qur'an means to **recite**. Page 62 tells you how Muhammad first had to learn the Qur'an by heart. Even today Muslims try to learn parts of the Qur'an by heart. Children aged six years can learn small parts.

Some Muslims learn the whole book by heart. A person who can recite the whole Qur'an is called a Hafiz.

It is a blessing for a Muslim to hear the Qur'an being read.

Worship

Use of the Qur'an

Muslims try to read some of the Qur'an every day. They believe the book can help them with the **problems** they face in life. The Qur'an is also read at weddings and funerals. Words from the Qur'an are hung on the wall at home.

The Qur'an has 114 chapters. Each has a name and a number. The book can be divided into 30 equal pieces. Then it can be read in one month.

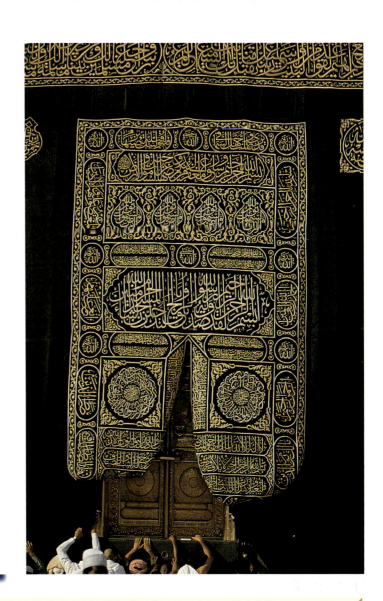

Passages from the Qur'an can be used to decorate objects. This material covers the Ka'bah at Makkah (see page 66).

Can you remember?

1 Muslims believe the Qur'an contains the _____ of Allah.

2 The Qur'an is stored on the _____ shelf.

3 The word Qur'an means to _____.

4 Muslims believe the Qur'an can help them with their everyday _____.

Do you know?

Can you list three ways in which Muslims take special care of the Qur'an?

2.4 Extension tasks

1 Daily Prayer times

Fajr –   around dawn.
Zuhr –   between noon and mid afternoon.
Asr –   between mid afternoon and just before sunset.
Maghrib – between sunset and dark.
Isha –   during darkness and before dawn.

Look at these prayer times above. Would a Muslim pupil in your class be able to say all the prayers? Is there time for them to prepare for prayer?

2

'I don't see why you make such a fuss about a book. There are loads of books in the world.'

What would a Muslim say?

3

- Name each thing the arrows point to.
- Can you write a sentence about each one?
- Design your own prayer rug. Page 25 will help you.

26 Worship

4 Make a poster to put in the washroom at the mosque. It is to teach children about washing before prayer. You will need a sentence telling them why it is important to do this.

5 This is an Islamic compass. Why do you think a Muslim needs a compass for prayers?

6 Your School Council has been asked to help Muslim pupils and teachers with their prayers.
- What changes need to be made to the buildings?
- What timetable changes would help?

7 Write a leaflet to go in a box with the Qur'an. It must tell teachers:
- how to store the book.
- how to respect the book.

8 a) How many times a day does a Muslim pray?
   b) Why does a Muslim use a rug?
   c) Why are the prayer positions called rak'ahs?

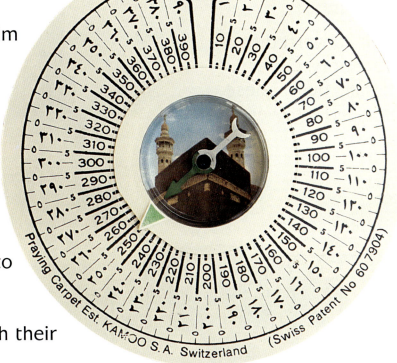

3.1 The mosque outside

What is a mosque?

The word mosque means to **bow** low. Muslims bow low to show that Allah is the greatest.

Any place where a Muslim **prays** is a mosque. It does not have to be a special building. Muhammad said it is more important to pray at the right time. Prayer can be at home. Then home is a mosque.

Some mosques are converted from buildings that are empty. Other mosques are specially built. These often have a dome and a tower.

This new mosque in Birmingham is said to be the largest in Europe. The dome roof makes this mosque easy to spot. The tower is called a minaret.

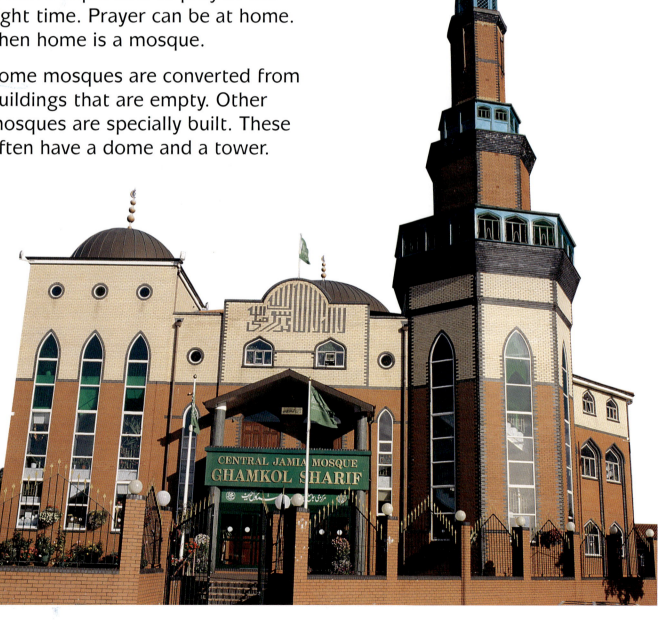

The dome

A **dome** helps to keep the room cool. This is important in a desert country. The dome also makes it easier to hear the teacher's voice. The shape reminds Muslims of the universe made by Allah.

The minaret

The **minaret** is a tall tower. It is used to call people to prayer. Loudspeakers are often fixed to it. In Britain the call to prayer is only heard inside a mosque. But new mosques still have a minaret.

Use of the mosque

The mosque has lots of uses:
- a place of worship.
- a place for people to meet socially.
- a place to learn about Islam and Arabic.

The mosque is used every day. Prayers are said there five times each day. This makes the mosque a good meeting place for Muslims.

Can you remember?

1. The word mosque means to _____ low.
2. A Muslim _____ in the mosque.
3. Many mosques have a _____ that helps to keep the room cool.
4. The call to prayer can be heard from the _____ .

Do you know?

What sort of things would a Muslim learn at a mosque?

3.2 Mosque – prayer hall

This platform is used on Fridays. It is called a minbar. The imam sits here to teach people.

The **prayer** hall is the most important room. It has no seats. The floor is covered with carpet.

Can you remember?

1 The most important part of the mosque is the _____ hall.

2 One wall of the mosque faces _____.

3 The _____ on the mosque wall is from the Qur'an.

4 Men and women sit apart so they do not _____ each other from worship.

Do you know?

Which day of the week would a Muslim hear a talk given at the mosque?

Mosque

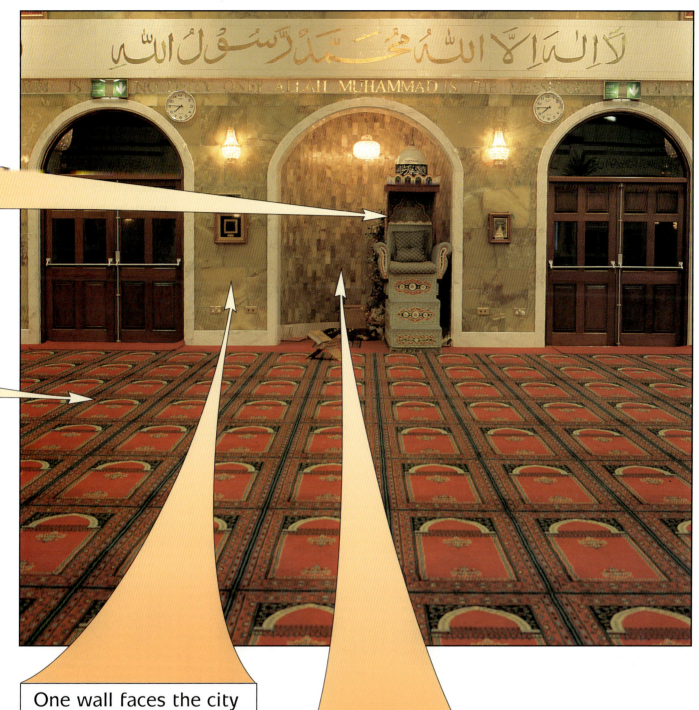

One wall faces the city of **Makkah**. There are no pictures of people or animals. This helps people to clear their mind and worship only Allah. The **writing** is from the Qur'an.

The alcove is shaped like an ear. It reminds Muslims that Allah hears their prayers.

If women go to the mosque they sit in the balcony. Men and women sit apart so they do not **distract** each other.

3.3 Other rooms at the mosque

Washing
Muhammad said, 'The key to Paradise is prayer and the key to prayer is cleanliness'. There are special places to **wash** in the mosque. There is one place for men and another for women. People sit on a stool and wash under running water.

Mosque school
Some big mosques have a special schoolroom. Muslims need to learn Arabic to read the Qur'an. **Children** go there for one or two hours every night after school. Adults also go to the mosque to learn about Islam.

32 Mosque

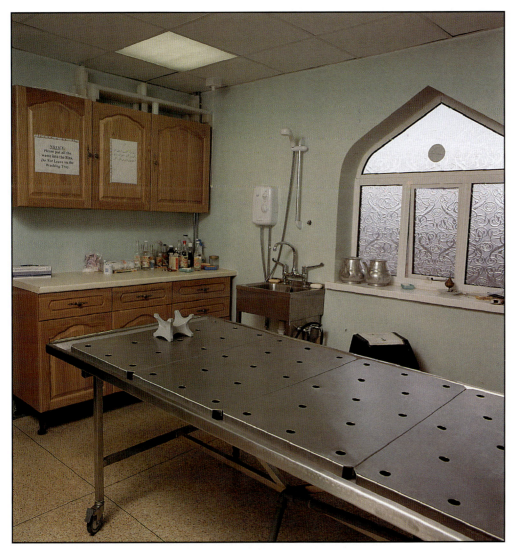

Mortuary

Some mosques have a special room to prepare a **dead** Muslim for burial. Members of the family can help. The body is carefully washed and dried. Then it is put in the coffin.

Other facilities

Muslims hold meetings at the mosque. There are rooms for family events. There is also a **library** of books about Islam.

Can you remember?

1 There is a special place to _____ before prayer at the mosque.

2 _____ go to mosque school to learn to read the Qur'an.

3 A _____ body can be washed at the mosque ready for burial.

4 Muslims can read books on Islam in the _____ at the mosque.

Do you know?

Name three rooms you might find at a big mosque.

3.4 People at the mosque

The imam

Everybody is equal. There are no priests in Islam. But Muslims think it helps if a man leads the prayers. He is called the **imam**. The imam knows a lot about Islam.

The imam's job is to:

- **Lead the community**
  The imam can talk to the newspapers or to the police. He may visit a Muslim in hospital. Or he may help them with **personal** problems.

- **Teach**
  The imam gives lessons to all ages. He can teach children Arabic. He teaches people how to live a good life.

- **Lead the prayers**
  The imam stands at the front in the prayer hall. He **leads** the prayers five times a day. He also gives a talk about Islam at Friday prayers. This is called a sermon.

At Friday prayers the imam teaches people more about Islam.

Muezzin

The muezzin **calls** people to prayer. In Muslim countries he climbs a tower. Then his voice can be heard clearly. In Britain he stands in the prayer hall. His voice is heard on the loudspeaker all round the mosque. People know they must get ready to pray.

This muezzin is calling Muslims to prayer from the top of a minaret in an Islamic country.

Can you remember?

1. The leader of the Muslim community is called the _____.
2. He can help Muslims with _____ problems.
3. The imam _____ the prayers.
4. The muezzin _____ Muslims to prayer five times a day.

Do you know?

How could the imam help Muslims?

3.5 Extension tasks

1. Write an advert for a muezzin's job. What sort of person would be best for this job? Does he need a good voice? Can he keep good time? Can a woman do the job?

Saddam picks French for his giant mosque

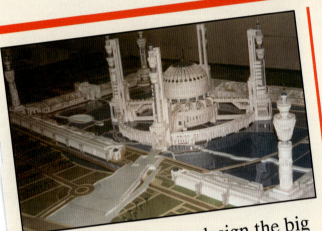

A Frenchman is to design the big mosque for President Saddam Hussein. The new mosque will be the biggest mosque in the world.

Jacques Barriere is the architect. Daniel Ganichaud is the engineer. The new mosque will have space for 45,000 people to worship.

It will have eight minarets or towers. That is one more than the Grand Mosque in Makkah. The tallest tower is to be 820ft.

The mosque will be built on an old airfield. The site is 75 acres. It is on the banks of the river Tigris.

The main building is circular. It will be 650ft in diameter. The dome in the centre will be 230ft high.

The mosque buildings will have a large lake built around them.

2.
   a) Why will this mosque be special?
   b) How many towers will it have?
   c) How many towers does the mosque at Makkah have?
   d) How many Muslims will be able to worship at the new mosque?

3 What do the arrows point to? Write one sentence about each feature.

4 Match each word to its correct meaning.

Mosque	the platform used by the imam to give his talk.
Minaret	the place where Muslims worship.
Makkah	the tower where the call of prayer is made.
Minbar	the holiest city for Muslims.

5 Your firm has been asked to look at a church that is for sale. It could be made into a mosque. Write to Mr Khan.
- Tell him what will have to be taken out of the church to make a mosque.
- You could include a quick sketch.

6 In pairs or groups of three design your own mosque.
- Draw the outside. Label it.
- Make a plan of the inside.
- Label the prayer hall, the schoolroom, the places to wash for prayer, the library and a room for meetings.

7

Try this role play:

A radio interviewer talks to the imam. She asks him to tell people about his job. Many of the listeners are not Muslims. What will she ask?

4.1 Family life

An extended family includes grandparents, aunts, uncles and cousins.

Muslims think the family matters. It is the basis of society. Home is where you learn how to look after yourself and how to behave. Muslims believe Allah **created** the family.

One big family

In Islam your family is **everyone** who is related to you. Some can be distant relatives. Muhammad said the best people look after those in their family.

The duties of parents

Mothers must look after their children. Muhammad said a mother should be a good **friend** to her children. She must be loving and fair. The father's job is to provide things for the children. They must not go without food, clothes and items they really need.

The parents' jobs may look different. But Islam says that a mother and father are equal. Both have important things to do for their children. In the home the children learn their religion. Their parents show them how to behave by setting a good example. Children are taught how to pray. They also learn pieces from the Qur'an. Parents should care for their children until marriage.

Living Islam

The duties of children

Everybody is somebody's child. Muslims say you have a duty to your parents all your life. Children must always **obey** their parents. It doesn't matter how old they are. Children must also show their parents respect because they are older and wiser.

Islam says that service to Allah comes first. Service to your parents comes next.

Muslims think it is wrong to put an old person in a home. They believe old people must be loved and cared for by their children. That is fair. The parents cared for the children when they were helpless. Brothers and sisters have to look after each other too.

This English woman married the cricketer Imran Khan. She became a Muslim. Mrs Jemima Khan says that Muslim children are looked after by everyone in the family.

Can you remember?

1 Muslims believe that the family was _____ by Allah.

2 In Islam your family includes _____ who is related to you.

3 A Muslim mother should be a good _____ to her children in Islam.

4 Children must respect and _____ their parents all their life.

Do you know?

What sort of things do children learn in a Muslim home?

4.2 Halal and Haram

Halal

Halal means something which is **good** for a Muslim to do. It might be food they can eat. It could be how they should dress.

What clothes are halal?

A Muslim should dress **modestly**. Their clothes should be suitable for prayer. That means Muslims must not wear clothes to make people look at them. Clothes should cover the body from neck to ankles. They should not cling. They should not be see-through. Muslim women also cover their hair when they go out.

What food is halal?

Muslims think food is a gift from Allah. This means it should be prepared with care. Muslims thank Allah for the food before they eat it.

The food we eat builds our body. That makes it very important. The Qur'an has rules about which food is best to eat. This food is halal.

Haram

Haram means it is forbidden. This may be food or clothing that is not decent.

This Muslim couple are dressed modestly. Their clothes are halal.

Living Islam

What food is haram?

Most food is good for a Muslim to eat. But the Qur'an says some meat is not.

A Muslim must not eat:
- any food made from a **pig**.
- the meat of an animal which eats other animals.
- any animal that has not been killed properly. A Muslim butcher must cut the animal's throat and say the name of Allah. The blood is drained away.

Muslims are not allowed to drink alcohol. This is because people can cause trouble when they are drunk.

What is wholesome to eat is halal. Most food is halal. Muslims buy meat from a halal butcher. They are sure it has been prepared correctly.

Can you remember?

1. Halal means something which is _____.
2. Something which is not good for a Muslim is called _____.
3. Muslims must dress _____ and not draw attention to themselves.
4. Any meat from a _____ cannot be eaten by Muslims.

Do you know?

What sort of clothes are halal for a Muslim woman to wear?

4.3 Ramadan

What is Ramadan?

Ramadan is the name of a **month**. It is also the fourth pillar of Islam. Muslims should fast for the whole month of Ramadan. That is 30 days.

Fasting

In Ramadan Muslims do not eat or drink in **daylight**.

Muslims fast to **obey** Allah. Fasting is a test of will power. Muslims say if they can fast, then they can do anything.

Fasting makes Muslims equal. Even a rich person must fast. Money is given to the poor at Ramadan.

Reading the Qur'an

Ramadan is a holy time. Allah gave the Qur'an in Ramadan (see page 62). Muslims spend time reading the **Qur'an**. They pray more and go to the mosque.

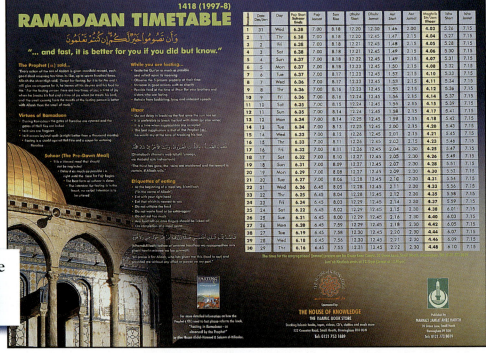

Muslims use a timetable to tell them when the fast starts and finishes.

42 Living Islam

Ramadan is fun!

That might not sound true. Yet Muslims are really pleased if they have kept the fast. The evening meal is a very happy time. They enjoy their food and want to share the meal with friends.

Not everybody must fast. Children under 12 years do not have to fast. But many children try to fast for a few days. Nobody who is ill must fast. The Qur'an says, 'Allah does not want to put you to difficulties'.

This family ends the fast with an evening meal together.

Can you remember?

1. Ramadan is the name of a _____ when Muslims fast.
2. They do not eat or drink in the _____.
3. By fasting Muslims are showing they _____ Allah.
4. Ramadan is a time to study the _____.

Do you know?

Who does not have to fast?

4.4 Id

Id Mubarak!

Id means **festival**. Id Mubarak means 'Have a happy festival!' There are two main festivals in Islam. Id-ul-Fitr and Id-ul-Adha.

Id is a time when:
- families and friends meet.
- money and food are given to charity.
- people wear new clothes.
- people give cards and presents.
- people spend more time in prayer and Qur'an reading.

Id-ul-Fitr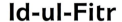

This Id is at the end of Ramadan. The festival starts when the new moon is seen.

The real celebrations begin the next day. Everyone puts on new clothes and goes to the mosque together. The **poor** are not forgotten. Money is collected for them. They will be able to enjoy the celebrations too. The rest of the day is spent visiting family and friends. People have a good time and eat a lot. Family graves are visited if possible.

These hands are decorated with henna for Id. This is called mendhi.

Everyone tries to attend prayers at Id. The mosque is usually crowded.

44 Living Islam

Id-ul-Adha

This Id is the more important festival. It comes at the time of the pilgrimage, Hajj (see page 66). **Adha** = sacrifice. Muslims remember when the prophet **Abraham** was tested by Allah. Abraham was asked to sacrifice his son. That was a hard test.

Abraham began to obey Allah. But Allah stopped him. Allah gave him a ram instead.

Today Muslims sacrifice a sheep. In Britain they pay to have the animal killed for them. The meat is shared. Some is given to the poor and some is cooked for the meal.

These girls are choosing posters to decorate their school for Id.

Can you remember?

1. The word Id means _____.

2. Muslims remember the _____ at Id by giving them money and meat.

3. There are two Ids but Id-ul-_____ is the more important one.

4. An animal is sacrificed at Id-ul-Adha to remember how _____ was tested by Allah.

Do you know?

Can you think of three things families do at Id?

45

4.5 Concern for others

> He is not a believer who eats his fill while his neighbour remains hungry by his side.

Muslims believe that Allah **decides** who will be rich and who will be poor. It is not wrong to have money. But it is a test. Muslims believe Allah watches how a person uses their money. He will **reward** the generous. He will punish the greedy.

Every Muslim should help other people, Muslim or not. Even a poor person can say a kind word or help someone.

Zakah

The third pillar of Islam is called zakah. It is a **2.5**% tax Muslims pay on their money. The money is used to help special Muslim causes. Muslims believe they must pay zakah. It will purify the rest of their money for them to enjoy.

Give a donation!

Muslims give other money to charity. They may put coins in a tin to help the hospital. Or give a large gift to a disaster fund.

Muslims have organised lots of charities. The Red **Crescent** is the Muslim part of the Red Cross. The two work together to help anyone in need in the world.

Money is given to the poor to thank Allah for the birth of a baby. It is also given at Id.

Muslims are ready to help in an emergency.

Can you remember?

1 Muslims believe Allah _____ who is to be rich and who is to be poor.

2 Allah will _____ people who are generous.

3 Muslims should pay _____ % as zakah.

4 Red _____ is the name of a well-known Muslim charity.

Do you know?

What do Muslims think happens to the rest of their money if they pay zakah?

4.6 Extension tasks

1. Design a menu for an Id party. Put it on an A4 sheet with decorations. Do not draw any people or animals on it. Your menu can have any food you like. But the food must be halal.

2.
Draw round your hand. Decorate this with a pattern that could be used for mendhi. A brown or orange colour would be best. The hands could be used on a group poster about Id.

3. Check the Internet site www.holidays.net/ramadan for details of the fast. Or you could look at www.salaam.co.uk for more information about Islam. You can send an e-mail Id Card from www.muslimdirectory.co.uk.

4. Copy out four sentences below that are true.

    a) The father is the most important person in a Muslim family.
    b) Id comes at the end of Ramadan.
    c) It is haram for a Muslim to eat pork.
    d) Muslims are only allowed to give money to help other Muslims.
    e) Id-ul-Adha is a more important festival than Id-ul-Fitr.
    f) A Muslim must give 2.5% of their money to charity.

5. **Halal school dinners!**

    Choose one of the following tasks:

    - Plan a packed lunch for a Muslim pupil.
    - Look at today's school dinner. Choose the food that would be halal for a Muslim pupil.

Living Islam

6 How would a Muslim answer this letter in the newpaper?

> page 14 MUSLIM TIMES
>
> 'I love animals. I don't see why they should be killed at Id-ul-Adha.'
>
> Signed
>
> An animal lover

7 Design your own pop-up Id card.
- You will need glue and felt pens.
- Write **Id Mubarak!** inside.

8 Match each word on the left to its correct meaning on the right.

Ramadan	food a Muslim can't eat.
Halal	money given to charity.
Zakah	food a Muslim can eat.
Haram	the month a Muslim fasts.

9

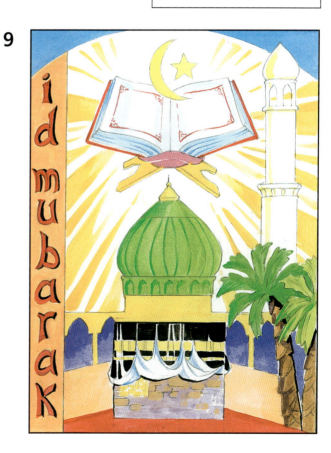

What pictures can you see on this Id card? Which Id do you think the card is for?

5.1 Birth ceremonies

First words

Muslims believe that babies are a **gift** from Allah. The first word a baby hears should be Allah – the name of God. Soon after birth, the father picks up the new baby. Sometimes another male relation will do this. He **whispers** in the baby's ear 'Allahu Akbar'. That means 'God is greatest'.

A sweet life

Someone often puts something sweet, like honey, on a new baby's gums. They also say a blessing. They hope the baby will be sweet and please Allah.

A baby boy is circumcised in hospital. This means the foreskin of the penis is taken off. This is because God told prophets in the past to do this.

Muhammad said, 'Pronounce as the first words to your child that there is no God but Allah'.

50 Rites of passage

Shaving the head

A baby is welcomed home with a special party. This takes place on the seventh day after birth. It is called **Aqiqah**.

The baby's hair is carefully shaved off. It is weighed. An equal weight in gold or silver is given to **charity**.

An animal is sacrificed to thank God for the baby. One sheep is killed for a girl and two for a boy. Some of the meat is given to the poor and some to friends. The rest is cooked for the party.

Hair is shaved off as a sign of purity. After it is weighed, the hair is buried in the earth.

Naming

Everyone is told the baby's name. The baby may be called after a famous Muslim in history. Or it could be given one of the 99 names of Allah (see page 9).

Can you remember?

1. Muslims believe babies are a _____ from Allah.
2. Soon after birth a man _____ the name of Allah in the baby's ear.
3. The hair is weighed and money is given to _____.
4. The baby is named at the _____ ceremony.

Do you know?

How do Muslims thank Allah for their baby?

5.2 Marriage – preparation

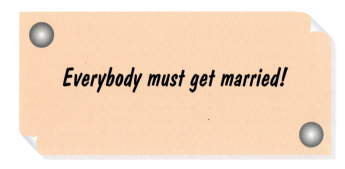

Everybody must get married!

Marriage is most important in Islam. The Qur'an says all **Muslims** must get married. No one should have sex before marriage.

Blood is thicker than water!

Some people say this. It means your family is more important than your friends. People in a family will always care for each other. They may help each other out with money. They will look after a relative who is ill.

Islam says marriage joins two **families**. They share the good times. They will also help each other in hard times.

Mum knows best

Families **arrange** their child's marriage. Muslims say your parents know you best. They also say that love and romance don't always last. It is not the basis for a lasting relationship.

Parents look for a match for their child. They arrange a meeting between the boy and girl. If the couple like each other they can meet again. If they do not, the wedding is cancelled. The parents must look again. The Qur'an says no one must be forced into marriage.

Four wives

A Muslim man can have up to **four** wives at the same time. But he must treat them equally. He may want another wife if the first one can't have a baby. Some say it is better to marry another woman than to have an affair. Most Muslim men do not have more than one wife. A Muslim woman can only have one husband. In Britain a Muslim man can only marry one woman.

This Muslim leader is the Sultan of Brunei. He presented his two wives to the Queen when he visited Britain.

Can you remember?

1 The Qur'an says all _____ must marry.

2 In Islam a marriage joins two _____ as well as two people.

3 Muslim parents _____ a marriage because they believe they know their children well.

4 A Muslim man can marry _____ wives if he can treat them equally.

Do you know?

Why do Muslims say it may be kinder for a man to have two wives?

5.3 Marriage – ceremony

The mahr

The groom gives his future wife some money before they marry. This is called the **mahr**. It shows he can **afford** to keep her and their children. Part of the money can be given as jewellery. Some of the money may be kept back. The wife is given the rest if the couple ever divorce. It will help her pay for a new home.

The nikah

When the money is agreed, a **contract** is signed. This is called a nikah. It says how much money the groom is giving. The girl can also say that she is to be the only wife, if she wishes.

The groom signs the nikah. The bride lets her father sign it for her. Two men sign the contract as witnesses. The signing can take place anywhere. It may be at home. Once the nikah is signed the couple are married. In Britain they also need a civil ceremony at a Register Office.

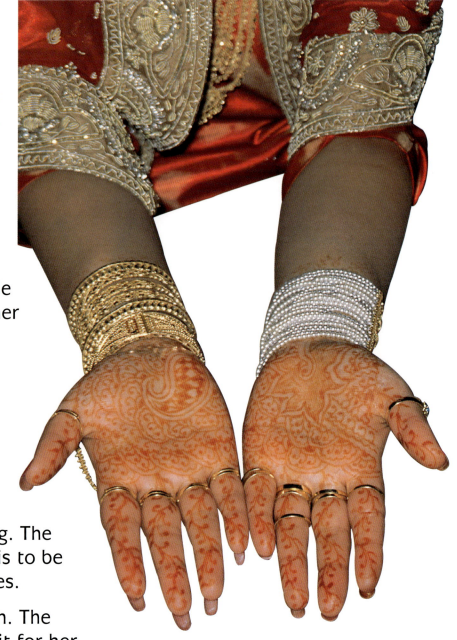

This bride's hands have been painted with henna ready for the walimah.

54 Rites of passage

The walimah

After the contract has been signed, there is a wedding reception. This is called a **walimah**. Families and friends get together for a party. The men meet in one room and the women in another.

People like to dress up for this. Many Asian brides wear a red or pink dress. The groom may wear a special head-dress.

This couple wear the traditional wedding clothes of Pakistan. A Muslim couple can wear whatever they choose.

Can you remember?

1 The bridegroom gives his wife some money called the _____.

2 This shows that he can _____ to keep her and their children.

3 The nikah is a marriage _____ which is signed by the groom and bride's father.

4 The reception where the families meet to celebrate is called a _____.

Do you know?

Why is a Muslim bride given jewellery?

5.4 Death, funerals and mourning

> From the earth We have created you, and to the earth We will restore you: And from it We will bring you back to life.

Care of the dying

Someone will try to **stay** with a person who is dying. They read the Qur'an to them. They will also help them confess their sins and comfort them. Muslims hope the name of Allah is the **last** word they hear as they die.

After death the body is washed. It is wrapped in a plain white cloth. If the Muslim has been on the pilgrimage their special clothes are used (see page 65). The body is put in a simple coffin. The head is turned to face the holy city of Makkah.

The coffin of Dodi Al Fayed is covered by a cloth with writings from the Qur'an. He was killed in a car crash with Diana, Princess of Wales. He was buried within 24 hours of his death.

56 Rites of passage

Funeral

A funeral is held as soon as possible. The coffin is taken to the mosque for prayers. After prayers there is a burial. The body must go back into the **earth**. It cannot be burned.

Muslims believe Allah will join the body and soul again in the future.

Mourning

The family stay at home for seven days after the funeral. Friends visit to offer comfort. They also read the Qur'an with them. Children have a duty to **pray** for the souls of their parents.

Muslim graves are plain and simple. This shows that everyone is equal in the sight of Allah.

Can you remember?

1 Someone will always _____ with a dying person to comfort them.

2 A Muslim hopes the _____ word they hear as they die will be the name of Allah.

3 A Muslim's body must go back into the _____ and cannot be cremated.

4 Children must _____ for the soul of a dead parent.

Do you know?

What do Muslims believe will happen to the body and soul?

5.5 Extension tasks

1

Try one of these role plays:

- A radio interviewer asks a Muslim boy why his parents will choose a wife for him.

- Imagine you have to telephone the cemetery. You are a Muslim who needs to arrange a funeral for a relative.

2 Write a short story. The title is 'I'll look out for you!'

The story is about a family. They have moved to a new area. The family looks after each other.

3 In groups of three or four make a poster. It must show the different parts of a Muslim wedding. You will need to use symbols and words because you can't draw people on it.

4 Write two sentences about this girl's wedding.

5 Design a card for the parents of a new baby girl.

6 Research five possible names for a Muslim boy and five names for a girl. (Hint: find out the names of Muhammad's wives, daughters and friends.)

58 Rites of passage

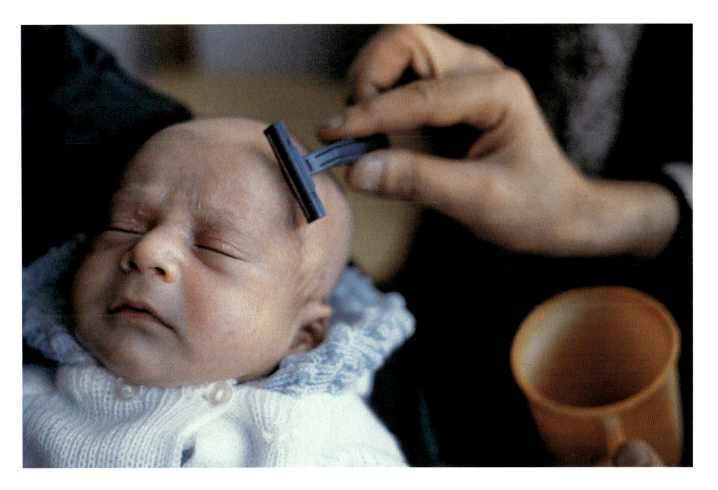

7 Write two sentences about this picture above. What is happening to the Muslim baby? Why?

8 Class discussion:

Should you listen to your parents when you choose whom to marry?

9 a) How does a Muslim care for someone who is dying?
b) Which way is the head turned in the coffin?
c) Where is the coffin first taken?
d) Can Muslims be cremated?

10 Match the heads on the left with the correct tails on the right.

A forced marriage is	in the coffin.
A baby boy is circumcised	for their children to marry.
A Muslim is wrapped in a plain white cloth	at eight days old.
The parents find a person	not allowed in Islam.

6.1 Life of Muhammad

This says Muhammad in Arabic.

Marriage and family life

Khadijah was very impressed by Muhammad. She proposed marriage to him. He was 25 years old at this time.

Birth and childhood

Muhammad was a real person. He was born in **Makkah** in Saudi Arabia about 570 CE. He had a sad childhood. His father died before he was born. His mother died when he was six years. He was brought up by his uncle who was a **trader**.

Muhammad worked for his uncle buying and selling. He was known as an honest person. He went to work for a wealthy widow. She was called Khadijah.

Makkah is still a busy city today.

Muhammad was a very rich businessman but he was honest. He was angry with what he saw in Makkah. Many rich people treated the poor badly. Some people in Makkah worshipped statues. But Muhammad believed in one God. He did not know what to do. He often went up into the hills to think.

The prophet

One day in 610 CE Muhammad saw an angel. This angel gave him words from Allah. Muhammad became a messenger or **prophet**. Muhammad told his family and friends about it. He also began teaching the people of Makkah. But they did not want to hear. They kept attacking Muhammad.

The Hijrah

Muhammad gave up trying to help Makkah. He went to Madinah. The people there wanted him to come and teach them about Allah. This move to Madinah is called the **Hijrah**. It was the beginning of the spread of Islam.

Final years

Muhammad lived in Madinah for the rest of his life. He taught people how Allah wanted them to live. Muhammad died in 632 CE aged 63.

Can you remember?

1. Muhammad was born in _____ in 570 CE.
2. He worked for his uncle as a _____ and was known to be very honest.
3. Muhammad became a _____ when the angel brought him words from Allah.
4. The _____ is important because it is the beginning of the spread of Islam.

Do you know?

Why did Muhammad have to leave his home town of Makkah?

6.2 Receiving the Qur'an

The cave

Muhammad was 40 years old when he was given the first words of the Qur'an. One day in Ramadan in 610 CE he left the town to go and think. Muhammad sat on the side of a hill called Mount **Hira**. He fasted to clear his mind.

Read!

Muhammad sat in a cave. Suddenly an angel appeared. The angel said, 'Read in the name of your Lord who created!' Muhammad was terrified. He could not read. The angel squeezed him hard. Muhammad thought he would die. Three times the angel said, 'Read!' Suddenly Muhammad could say the words.

This is where Muhammad sat on Mount Hira. He had a vision of an angel in this cave.

The angel

'O Muhammad you are the messenger of Allah. I am **Jibril**', the angel said.

Muhammad ran home. He was in shock. He thought he was going mad. But his wife understood. She told him he was a messenger of Allah. Another name is a **prophet**.

The angel returned many times. Each time Muhammad was given messages from Allah. He learned them by **heart** and told his friends. They wrote everything down. They used anything they could find. Sometimes they wrote on dried leaves or dry bones.

Holy city of Makkah

Correct

Everything was written down carefully. It was read back to Muhammad. He checked it word by word. Muhammad did not want there to be any mistakes. The pieces were put together as a book. The book is called the Qur'an.

Some Muslims learn every word by heart. This takes great skill. A Muslim who knows the Qur'an by heart is called a Hafiz.

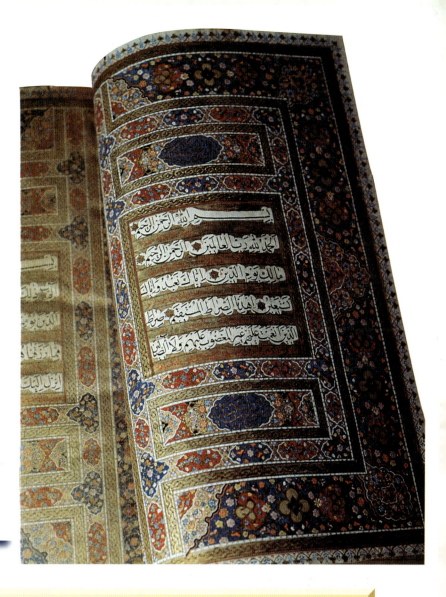

This is one of the oldest copies of the Qur'an. It is kept in Istanbul.

Can you remember?

1 Muhammad was given the words of God by the angel _____.

2 He was sitting in a cave on Mount _____ outside Makkah when this happened.

3 Because Muhammad could not read, he learned each piece by _____.

4 Muhammad's wife knew he was a _____ of Allah.

Do you know?

Who did Muhammad tell the words of the Qur'an to?

6.3 Hajj 1

What is Hajj?

Hajj = pilgrimage to Makkah. A **pilgrimage** is a journey to a holy place. This is for a religious reason. Hajj is the fifth pillar of Islam (see page 16). Every Muslim must go on Hajj once in their **life**. They are excused if they are ill or can't afford it.

Why?

- The Qur'an says a Muslim must go.
- Muhammad went on Hajj. Muslims copy what he did.
- Hajj is a **test** of what a Muslim will do for Allah.
- It makes a Muslim spiritually clean.
- They join two million other Muslims on Hajj. Muslims feel part of the brotherhood of Islam.

When?

A Muslim must go on Hajj between the 8th and 13th of the month of Dhul-Hijjah. If they go at a different time, it is not called Hajj.

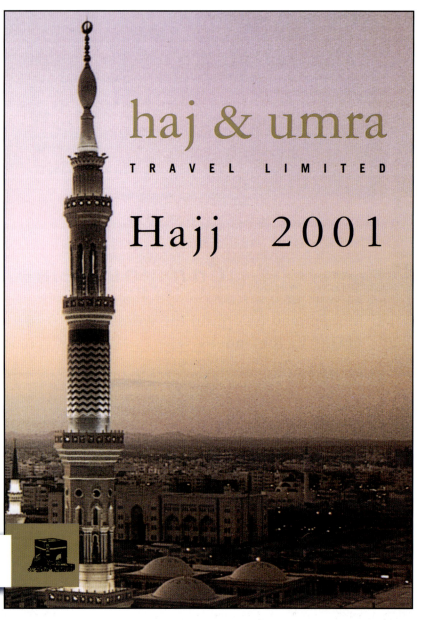

The pilgrimage to Makkah costs a lot of money.

Holy city of Makkah

Getting ready

Muslims have to book their travel. They also need a visa from the mosque. Only Muslims can go to the holy city of Makkah. No one else can enter. The clothes worn on Hajj are plain white cotton sheets. Everyone wears the same. This shows that rich and poor are equal. A pilgrim must be **pure** in mind and body for Hajj.

The pilgrim's clothes are called ihram. A man wears two pieces of white cloth without seams. A woman can wear ordinary clothes or five pieces of cloth.

Can you remember?

1 Hajj is the _____ Muslims make to Makkah.

2 All Muslims must go once in their _____ unless they are too ill or too poor.

3 Hajj is a _____ of what a Muslim will do for Allah.

4 A Muslim must be _____ in mind and body during Hajj.

Do you know?

Why do Muslims wear ihram?

6.4 Hajj 2

Seven times round the Ka'bah
Pilgrims walk seven times **round** the Ka'bah. The Ka'bah is the cube-shaped building in the centre of the mosque.

Running between two hills
Pilgrims run between two hills. These hills are covered by a corridor. They remember how Hajar, Abraham's wife, looked for water for her baby. **Allah** made a spring of water appear by the baby's heel. This is called the well of Zamzam.

Can you remember?

1. Muslims begin Hajj by going seven times _____ the Ka'bah in the big mosque.

2. The well of Zamzam was made by _____ to give water to Hajar's baby.

3. _____ is important because Muhammad preached his last sermon there.

4. Muslims _____ an animal and stone three pillars at Mina.

Do you know?

What does the Ka'bah look like?

Holy city of Makkah

Arafat
Pilgrims walk 13 miles to Arafat. They pray here like Muhammad did. He preached his last sermon at **Arafat**. Muslims collect 49 stones for the next day.

Mina
Muslims throw the stones at three pillars to stone the devil. At Mina, Muslims **sacrifice** an animal. They remember the story of Abraham's sacrifice (see page 45). Muslims show God they are willing to make a sacrifice themselves.

Finally, Muslims return to Makkah. They circle the Ka'bah to finish Hajj.

6.5 Extension tasks

1. Use a clean page in your exercise book. Display the main events in the life of Muhammad. Decorate the borders with the symbol of Islam.

2. Research in the library or on the Internet.
   - What can you discover about the size of Makkah and Madinah today?
   - Which airport would pilgrims from Britain use?
   - How does Makkah cope with the big numbers at Hajj?

3. Copy this map into your book. Write a sentence about what happens at each place.

4. Copy out the three correct statements below.
   a) Muhammad was a rich businessman.
   b) He was given a book with the Qur'an written in.
   c) His mother taught him to read.
   d) Muhammad saw an angel.
   e) Muhammad died in Madinah.

5. Make a diagram about the Qur'an in your book. You will need to draw a Qur'an on a stand in the centre (see page 12). Show how the Qur'an was given. Show how it is respected.

6. In groups of three or four make a poster about Hajj.
   - What does a pilgrim do at each place?
   - How do Muslims dress?

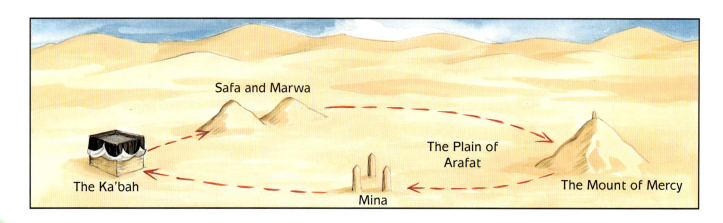

Holy city of Makkah

7 Write a caption to go under this picture. Write no more than 100 words.

8 This is the outside of a Muslim's house. He has been on Hajj. How do you know?

9 Match each word to its correct meaning.

Qur'an	was an angel.
Hijrah	was the name of Muhammad's first wife.
Khadijah	is the book containing the word of God.
Jibril	is the time when Muhammad left Makkah for Madinah.

Glossary

A
Akhirah life after death.
Alcove the part of the mosque facing Makkah.
Allah the Arabic name for God.
Allahu Akbar means God is greatest.
Aqiqah the ceremony seven days after the birth of a baby.
Arabic the language used in Islam.
Arafat a place visited by pilgrims on Hajj.
Asr prayers between mid-afternoon and sunset.

C
Charity giving money to the poor. It is the third pillar of Islam.
Circumcision the operation to remove the foreskin of a baby boy's penis.
Compass shows the direction of Makkah.

D
Day of Judgement Muslims believe Allah will judge them after death.
Dome a curved roof over a mosque.

F
Faith believing in Allah is the first pillar of Islam.
Fajr prayers around dawn.
Fasting Muslims do not eat or drink in daylight in Ramadan.
Five pillars the five basic beliefs of Islam.

H
Hafiz a person who can say the Qur'an by heart.
Hajar the wife of prophet Abraham.
Hajj the pilgrimage to Makkah.
Halal food or clothing which is proper for a Muslim.
Haram food or clothing which is wrong for a Muslim.
Hell a place where Muslims who have sinned go when they die.
Hijrah the time when Muhammad left Makkah for Madinah.

I
Id means festival.
Id Mubarak means 'Happy Festival!'
Id-ul-Adha the festival of sacrifice.
Id-ul-Fitr the festival at the end of Ramadan.

Ihram white clothing worn on Hajj.
Imam the leader of the Muslim community.
Isha prayers between dusk and dawn.
Islam the name of the religion. It means submission to Allah.

J
Jesus was an important prophet in Islam.
Jibril the angel who brought the Qur'an.

K
Ka'bah the holy place in the centre of Makkah.
Khadijah the wife of Muhammad.

M
Madinah the holy city where Muhammad lived and died.
Maghrib prayers between sunset and dark.
Mahr the dowry paid by the bridegroom to his wife.
Makkah the holiest city in Islam where Muhammad was born.
Mina a place pilgrims visit on Hajj.
Minaret the tower at a mosque, used to call Muslims to prayer.
Minbar where the imam sits to preach at Friday prayers.
Mortuary a room in a mosque used to prepare a body for burial.
Mosque the place of worship for Muslims.
Mount Hira where Muhammad received the Qur'an.
Muezzin the man who calls Muslims to prayer.
Muhammad the last and most important prophet in Islam.
Muslim a person who obeys Allah.

N
Nikah the marriage contract.

P
Paradise where Muslims hope to go after they die.
Pbuh means 'Peace be upon Him' and is used to show respect to a prophet.
Pilgrimage a special journey to Makkah also called Hajj.
Prayer the second pillar of Islam and must be performed five times a day.
Prophet a messenger from Allah.

Q
Qur'an the Muslims' holy book.

R
Rak'ah one of the prayer positions.
Ramadan the month when Muslims fast.
Red Crescent the Muslim branch of the Red Cross.

S

Saudi Arabia the country where Muhammad lived.

W

Walimah a Muslim wedding reception.

Wudu the special washing before prayer.

Z

Zakah the 2.5% payment to charity, the third pillar of Islam.

Zamzam a spring of water and a well in Makkah.

Zuhr prayers between noon and mid-afternoon.